Undressing the Earth

Undressing the Earth

poems

Becky Dennison Sakellariou

Kelsay Books

© 2018 Becky Dennison Sakellariou. All rights reserved. This material may not be reproduced in any form, published, reprinted, recorded, performed, broadcast, without the express written consent of Becky Dennison Sakellariou. All such actions are strictly prohibited by law.

ISBN 978-1-949229-09-7

Cover design by Shay Culligan

Acknowledgments

"Hell did not fall from the sky," from the anthology, *Carrying the Branch: Poets in Search of Peace,* edited by Diane Frank, Lois P. Jones, Rustin Larson, Gloria Mindock, and Melissa Studdard, Glass Lyre Press, 2017.

"White Matter," *Passager,* July, 2011

"Weather Reports," "Things Calling Me Away," "Neutrinos II," "Departure and Arrival," "Netted Bodies," *"Hell did not fall from the sky,"* featured on the website *Off the Margins*, under the name, Becky Dennison Sakellariou, edited by Maura MacNeil, spring 2017

to those who survived the crossing
to those who died in the water
to those who held the bleeding bodies
to those who bled themselves
to those who cannot stop weeping
to those who cannot weep

to those who do not understand
to those who do

*You, sent out beyond your recall,
go to the limits of your longing.
Embody me.*

Book of Hours, I, 59, Rainer Maria Rilke, trans, Joanna Macy

*There must be those with whom we can sit down and weep
and still be counted as warriors.*

Adrienne Rich, *Sources*

Contents

Salted Wounds	13
The Sleeping God	15
Hell did not fall from the sky	16
Undressing the Earth	18
Things Are Calling Me Away	20
Living with Fruit	21
Eggs and Grief	23
On Becoming Seventy	24
Impossible Cards	27
The Vocabulary of Friends	29
Departure and Arrival	31

♈

Prayer for Night Mercies	35
Netted Bodies	36
This One is for Joy	37
I thought I saw a doe	38
Late Afternoon in August	39
Weather Report	41
Neutrinos II	43
Slope and Aspect	45

♈

The Center of All Things	51
You, Then, Later	52
This object has been temporarily removed	54
As Good a Time as Any	56
Before You Could Speak	58
White Matter	60
The Fugue	61

About the Author

Salted Wounds

Something happened in the world today

A husband died and a woman cleaned out his closets
giving bags of trousers, shoes, pullovers
to the Afghan refugee camp

where the rats and snakes
had gotten into the moldy, damp room
filled with men's clothes saved over the summer
for sorting when the weather got cooler.

Something happened in the world today

A drone arrived in Ireland from Scotland
filled with birth control pills for the women

who swallowed them publicly
to protest the anti-abortion laws.

Something happened in the world today

A young girl watched a young man
slit her mother's throat in their kitchen,

his face covered with a dirty brown cloth,
eyes following her the whole time.

Something happened in the world today

A double rainbow appeared over a field of sheep
in the northeast, a child saw it
and believed she could touch it.

A woman is making fig jam and has forgotten to put
on her apron, but the sun is streaming into the kitchen
and she secretly licks her fingers.

A man is using the washing machine for the first time,
his fingers wandering over the symbols on the dial
as if he were reading Braille.

Something happened in the world today

A young boy looks at a young girl
and wants to be close to her
but his father will whip him if he tries.

A woman far away is folding and unfolding
a tablecloth embroidered in red and gold,
unable to decide whether to put it away.

A little boy looks out the window of his father's car
along Route 3, sees a sign, "Duck Crossing,"
and cries to his father *please stop please.*

I cannot hold it all.

The Sleeping God *

Today, January 28, 2015, 20 boats landed on the northern coast of the island of Lesbos, Greece, carrying a total of 1080 people. So far in 2015, just 28 days, at least 224 men, women and children have died trying to reach Europe via Turkey. That is 8 human beings each day.

The sleeping God never woke
when the boats broke apart
on the jagged rocks of Koufonisi.

This God never woke when the woman
who had never known water,
plunged into the black seas,
her blue-lipped children
coiling downward beside her
like dolls wrapped in burial clothes.

What was this God dreaming of
when this happened?
Was this Our God?
Do we *know* this God?

Did their God go under with them?
Did he pray with them as they sank?
Did he lay the cold babies alongside
their mother in the seabed?
Did he keen, sway, sounding the waves
they could not see through?

What was this God dreaming of
while they were drowning?

*phrase borrowed from Annie Dillard

Hell did not fall from the sky

after Paris

Hell did not fall from the sky
this time.

It arrived in human form,
black and furious,

aimed at our breasts,
our foreheads, our spirits.

The city wept
trapped inside the evacuation of color,

blackbirds gathering soundlessly along St. Anthony's
curved gold and marble spires,

our beards turning suddenly gray
like the wasted desert sands.

*

Why, then, was everything I saw today
filled with wonder?

At dusk, water fell from the heavens
and washed the blood

from the bodies, leaving them clean, curled, quiet,
as if just born.

The ribbed clouds released a band of last minute sun
illuminating our wet, scared faces

and a lullaby leaked from the edge
of shattered cobblestones.

Like the trout who thrives not in confinement
but in rushing, roiling currents,

I shall live in the water from now on,
not in the fire.

I may drown, but I will not burn.

Undressing the Earth

Even the stones will rise up if you dare invade my country.
                                            Anonymous

I have left the dirt under my nails
from digging out the clover that blankets my garden
as once I left the sticky salt in my hair
after swimming in the Gulf of Evia,
a cross-section of all great oceans,
our beloved, black earth, bones dug in deep.

The ground around the earthquake-broken school buildings
was soaked with charred school bags, scorched shoes
strewn through the bricks and rubble —
all black and white now,
no more color.

I need to collect the children's names
make lists of ages, mothers, birthdays, shoe sizes *

The rocky shore of Samos
is scattered with abandoned orange life jackets,
pink backpacks, slit black rubber boat fragments,
a sandal with bloodied inner soles,
a soggy green blanket,
one lost doll.

The UN Commission on Missing Persons
continues to plow the fields in Turkish-occupied Cyprus,
bull-dozers flipping out human remains forty years later.
Mothers, grandfathers, sons permanently dressed in black,
new generations gathered around long tables
still negotiating with terror and blank words.

I planted two lemon seedlings today

even though Snowdon cannot come home

even though someone influential spoke way out of turn

even though the field hospitals are overflowing with bloody
    amputated limbs

even though the broken vase is more beautiful for being broken

even though this morning white almond petals covered my car

and I drove through town like a bride

peel away the surface
discover nakedness in the musty damp caverns
dive into your own body
weave these stories together
compose just one long note

                                   *Ai Weiwei

Things Are Calling Me Away

a story in the words of Azize, an Afghan refugee

Things. Water. Safety. Hunger. Home.
Away. Toward. Here.

Objects are gone. Water is nowhere.
The man at the border says:
...if the sea seems safe,
earth must be hell.

My name is Azize.

At night, a pain sits between my breasts,
the cartilage swollen, aching and aching.
Something is wrong with me. I cannot even touch it.

Safety meant our front door, always open,
clean floors, no confusion, my soft bed, the red chair.
I am hungry for my home.

A man pushes me up
against a stained concrete wall,
makes a small high yelp,
backs away.
I am wet where he was.

I am away from good things
that are no longer.

What does all this mean?
My heart does not open
at the sight of mountains.
My prayers are in black and white.

This is not home.
This is a place.

Living with Fruit

I look at my life like a landscape.   Oliver Sacks

The moon was mine tonight, a perfect scythe
suspended in the grandest space known,
a slice of matter faultlessly aligned
with the black and white tomcat
lying on my foot.

The man fell onto the rocky shore and wept, and we
shoveled cat shit from under Adele's bed.
My son reassured me that I could come back
but you have gone away. I cannot find you,
neither throat sound nor body shape.

The pomegranates are still butter yellow
streaked with darkening red,
soon to split open from the weight
of ripening seeds.

Here in the Mediterranean
the first flowers of the spring are always yellow.
Ants are emerging from their winter nests,
one or two wandering, radarless, around the sink.

The nurses in the transit medical tents
are asking for emergency birthing kits
for the Syrian and Afghan women
who suddenly let loose their tiny newborns
when they finally reach shallow waters.

I watched a woman talking
to the pears at the street market today.
I found a few fat black olives
on the hundred-year-old tree
bowing toward the sea
from my front yard.

I have wounded my body with my life.

Eggs and Grief

> *Give yourselves to the air, to what you cannot hold.*
>   Rainer Maria Rilke: *Sonnets to Orpheus,* Part 1, IV

No more melons in the market,
not the sweet, juicy, pale green ones
that I eat all summer.

My suitcases sit empty, yawning
at my panic at what to put in
and what to leave out.
Will I return by spring?
will I need two jackets? a second pair of black boots?

What remains
sits in still, muffled colors.

I have to go to the bank again,
then pick up some eggs
which I will hard-boil, stuff with herbs and olives
and take to Rena's house
for her Sunday Family Lunch.

What I give away keeps returning,
my breath captures it on the way out
and breathes it right back,
a loop of images. My eyes don't close.

I cannot let go of these men and women
who have become my people,
who live my heart, eat my bones.

On Becoming Seventy

Weeping, I walk through the customs gate
turning to wave to whomever has brought me here.

I weep again in my seat
as I watch the planes idling,

lining up, turning toward the runway
like great prehistoric behemoths

departing this earth before the great fire.

We rise up through the thick smoky-gray cloud,
a soggy, weighted overcoat thrown over London,

pierce it soundlessly like a giant, determined needle
bursting out onto an infinite plain of rippling
      violet clouds,

the sun on the far horizon
licking the waves like butter melting,

the crest of each golden wave pink,
lavender shadows spinning, beckoning,
no fanfare, the infinite.

This is what I want heaven to look like.

The uneven, schismatic patterns
rake through mountain ranges,

valleys that twist and speed through millennia
        of rock,
ice frozen into the high crevices even in July,

our glorious, beloved home.

I fly toward a country
of motionless, fading orange leaf-beds

collected at the bottom of new rain pools,
skeletal trunks of undressing ash, beech, maple,

early morning insubstantial ice in the bird bath,
piles of noisy, yellowing leaves calling
for the dog to leap into,

coming rains,
my boots in the dark closet.

I return to cows lying down in concert
in the fields,

grass moist under their bellies,
their ears soft, the wind gentle.

I weep for my precious sons,
to smell their man skin,
feel their rough cheeks,

hear their everyday pleasures and grief,
watch them kneel beside their children,

look gravely into their eyes
listening to their stories with intent.

I ask the sky: *how could this happen?*
how did they become not-me?

how could I be the I
who I am right now?
where am I going?

Impossible Cards

are those we cannot shuffle,
faces hard against the table top,
unbearable mysteries:
king of spades, his eye on
the queen of diamonds, four fives,
the beloved ace,

each one, a chronicle
of finger prints, birth cauls
and black rubber hoses,
each one containing you, me,
every grandmother, gambler, trapeze artist,
all those who have shadowed us,
who still hover around our shoulders.

Add to this the baggage
covered with torn and curling stickers, labels,
yellow, green, long out of date,
gone into exile, migration, pilgrimage,
whole galaxies telling endless secrets,
the humming harmonies that roll across
the sky's house spilling wet color
over the earth's hunger.

   **

Are you listening?
We will talk on this winter morning
when it is neither snowing nor not snowing,
you four thousand miles away on this,
the anniversary of our mother's death,
twenty years gone now

and we will do
what we always do
stay close
sweet talk
love each other's voices
speak some Greek
remember and remember

The Vocabulary of Friends

						*

The woman in the booth beside me
leans over to her friend, says something
about *moaning* as she struggles
to get her right arm
into the faux red leather jacket.
Her teeth aren't in straight,
she whistles when she speaks.

Her friend, who limps and lists
to the left, goes outside the bar to smoke.
She has one tooth
on the right side of her mouth
and announces, chuckling,
that she is seventy-three.

When she comes back in, she laughs
and tells her friend
she has been *moaning*
out on the sidewalk
in sympathy with her.
Her friend doesn't quite get it,
but she laughs, too,
because they know each other well.

						*

I too struggle with the meaning of words
thrown to the ground,
words like *forgiveness*: my brother
waiting for his sisters; *ice storm*:
a wonder of grass sculpted

into frozen spidery octopus forms;
seminola: no way to find it
in the green grocer's or
explain it to the eager manager.

Words are my business,
every morning I release them
into the sky, every evening,
they fall back, once again,
onto my tongue for retasting, retelling.

Departure and Arrival

Before I set off this time,
the marsh maples graciously turn
a few of their highest leaves red
now dropping around my feet
these we offer you until you return –

Throughout the marsh
slimy brackish water settles deep and still,
branches shaped like a man and a woman
entangled in the pool
above the falls we climb toward.

Water lilies scatter in the paused curves
like dancers waiting for their cues.
Flat boulders tether the rushing, rust-hued water.
You ask, *how long has it been like this?*

I arrive on the other side of the ocean,
south near other salted bodies of water
where men carrying their women,
wade through black waves, weeping
when they reach the sand.

Where, in their dreams, other men
still fight wars in Asia Minor,
wearing the wounds of never knowing why.
Where none of these men will ever sleep.

The seas have become the olive groves,
their leaves blowing through me, drowning me,
weaving silver through the air.
This time I have left nothing behind,
not even you, nor a memory
of what might not be there.

**

Wake me from this death walk,
this long sleep,
walk me into the night-blooming jasmine,
yellow as butter just churned.

Notice an indentation in the earth
beneath the stone steps where tiny green leaves
cling close to dead summer stalks
like just-wakened children
circling their mother's skirts.

Drink in the blood-red moon
leaking like a split pomegranate,
listen to the drying vine leaves
crackling in their conversations.

Stand beneath mauve-stained
God-hewn cliffs
that lean hungrily into the sea.

♈

Prayer for Night Mercies *

We are all just walking each other home.
                              Ram Dass

I think I am falling in love with the cellist.
How he folds his arms around the instrument,
cheek lightly against her neck,
eyes half closed, finger tips stroking her strings,
immersed and dreaming in her body.

How he listens as she vibrates,
a quiver that travels deep in his veins
as he holds her gently, a tremor
that tells him how he must move.
His face turns toward her body,
his sound merges with hers,
his own throat opens to her voice.

He wakes at night to whales calling his name,
carries his cello to a beach on the Mexican coast
where the females are gathering to give birth.

He listens, and hears their songs,
slowly begins to play with them,
whispering and humming, pulsing to the waves,
the sonic landscape rising and shuddering
through the giant wombs and ribcages
until neither human nor animal
can recognize the world as it had once been,
knows only that they have surpassed
all definition, all bodies,
all skies and waters, all Gods and Kings.

   *cello piece composed by Eugene Friesen

Netted Bodies

I will unspool each day

then thread & knit
each knot once again

restitching our bodies
into a thousand years

daylight
and liquidity

our skin woven
into nets of scent

their random radiance
daring remorse

still
we lament

our mouths pressed
against closed doors

yearning for a renaissance
that will consume us

your body
disappearing

This One is for Joy

I am not away from you
no space between our bodies
I am inside the body
of sudden February snow
falling tenderly
on bursting almond blossoms

I stretch across your back
warm and fecund
your moisture mine
I do not know distance

I fly leaving your real body behind
I fly beside the sun
and understand joy

such joy that miles below
the white cliffs shift and pulse
geography slipping east

I can have you
even without
your warming body

because I am the sour-cherry seedling
naked and tall holding
its new earth
trembling as the snow feathers
its young buds
in wanton recklessness

I thought I saw a doe

I thought I saw a doe
lying ahead of me on the path
late this afternoon.
I moved to the side where the snow
had not been trodden
so as not to startle her,
bowed my head to avoid
the pine branches leaning low
along the sides of the path,
heavy with new snow.
As I approached her,
I saw that she was just a tangle
of branches and dead leaves
in some sudden familiar shape,

and I wished it had been the doe,
lying with her back legs
curved beneath her, her eyes
slightly averted from my coming.
I would kneel on the wet ground
and carefully pick up one front hoof,
warming it with my breath
to loosen the balls of frozen ice
caught between her toes.
I would pick the bits of hard snow
out of their crevices and stroke
the soft fur covering the hoof.
Her head would slowly move toward mine
until her cool nose was leaning
against my cheek and we would
crouch motionless, our worlds momentarily
whispering the infinite, the possible.

Late Afternoon in August

Weary, past midnight, who are you searching for?
"Questions for the Moon," Ho Xuan Huong

Plane trees lean toward ghost water
paused in ripples of mud in the old canal.
We push through thickets of bamboo.

Cicadas sizzle in the heat,
cling upside down on the bark of trees,
dead by morning, skin stretched like transparent vests
between tiny sculpted bones.

Alone, a man,
arms and neck deep brown from the sun,
hoes rows of baby lettuces.
Nearby, a prickly pear tree.

Early Morning in February

Snow turning to rain after midnight...

I woke at three to thunder
in a sky sliced into light,
soaked in a sudden *February thaw.*

On the mountainsides, the seams
of new streams split, wheezing
out of their frozen winter beds,
mosses suddenly drenched.

...rain turned to snow
flashed over glassy rocks,
miniature pools filled with a musky rush.
Unripe chestnuts, smooth, rust-colored,
covered the trail in their nakedness,
no shells, no protection

from the silent, gold-hued cedar wax-wing
watching from the nearby fallen oak,
raw green mushrooms clinging to its bark.

I am searching for the other body.

Weather Report

1

Great slabs of veined ice
still rim the shoreline
of Lake Skatutakee in April
while we work in our shirtsleeves
to push the car out of the mud.

2

In pounding, bone chilling, Icelandic rain
thousands of feet above the roaring North Atlantic,
the female razorbill
balances her soft white feathery bottom
on her new brown-speckled egg.

3

We are soaked, shivering and spellbound.

4

Two ants, just emerged from their winter nests,
wander up and down the sink,
their radar seemingly still inoperative,
while field hospitals are overflowing
with amputated limbs.

5

I do not need to return
to the old gray, splintered dock
that tilted precariously into the pond
one August afternoon
in order to know
the damp afternoon sun
still on my neck, my shoulders,
the smell of the murky, brackish water
that circles and strokes my submerged fingers,
the old sadness of my heart.

6

Between September and October, the light
on my small Mediterranean island
changes from hot white to a pale yellow
that says, *yes*, you can go into the garden now,
bend and lift, weed and rake.

7

Insects keep track of polarized light,
loggerhead turtles know the magnetic field
and geese are good at path integration.
As they fold into my body's cavities,
they become the bodies of the world.

Neutrinos II

Once thought to travel at the speed of light, [we now know that neutrinos] drift through the earth and our own bodies like moonlight through a window.

If we have our feet on the ground,
what do we do with the sky?

Are we standing up to our knees
in blue or has our skin become the sky?

How do we walk with moonlight
drifting through our bodies?

Those headstrong little neutrinos have resurfaced,
this time as Nobel Prize material.

All along, we thought they had no mass
as they traveled through space
on their way to earth from the sun.

Now it has been discovered that they change
their identities on the way *like spies on the run.*
They *oscillate…* fancy that…
between 3 different *flavors: electron, muon and tau.*

Scientists are shamelessly in love with them.
They have been known to applaud with abandon
as these "tiniest quantities of reality ever imagined
by a human being" switch disguises on their way
to the Super-K detector under Mount Ikenoyama
in the Gifu Prefecture.

That must be why, sometimes out of the blue,
I feel so light, so buoyed, so slow-motion;
it must be the neutrinos as they *drift*
unimpeded, undetected
through my arms, my ribs, my toes
on their way to their ghost-like homes,
shy, elusive, shape-shifting cones of light
we must simply just love.

Slope and Aspect

Slope

A hillside: the angle of incline.

The hill behind our house, sweet, familiar, ancient.

Firefighters take note: the steeper the slope, the faster

a fire burns up the slope.

No fires here, too chilly and wet.

Slope increases radiation and convection.

*Tomorrow I will take Tim and our spaniel, Gertie,
for a walk.*

The steeper the slope, the greater the up-slope heat transfer.

My dreams always contain mountains and green growth.

The fire will burn hotter and hotter, faster and faster.

Only if...

Anything on the steep slope that burns

(It will never burn, do not say that again)

will roll downhill to start other ignitions.

What could roll down? the rabbit, the mole, the wild rose petals?

This slope has a 100% grade.

This seems sound.

We learn fire-behavior. Listen to the daytime winds

I do that better than anyone around here

as they move up the face of the slope

like bees resting.

During the night, they will move downhill

like liquorice.

Watch out for slope re-heating,

(like your body at 2 a.m.)

the fire would be backing into the upslope winds.

These instructions are taped to our refrigerator door
alongside a black and white photo of my mother,
my father grinning, three of their children sitting
cross-legged on the grass and a fourth
standing behind them.

Aspect

Aspect describes the direction

Look, look here, toward me

in which a slope faces

poured out for you

and relates to the degree of solar exposure.

Naturally. You don't have to spell it out, for God's sake.

Does this slope face north? is it cooler and moister

than those that face south?

Watch the sun and you will know the answer.

Check the vegetation, it will tell you something.

My moss, my bushes, my twisted, bent trees.

Don't forget the humidity,

the places I always pause, the branches I grab, the berries I pick,

lower fuel moisture, sparser and lighter fuel loadings.

I look up when I climb and down when I descend.

North aspects of slopes are more shaded and have

I will no longer listen to this.

♈

The Center of All Things

I found a heart by the side of the road
at the entrance to the forest.
It was still beating as it looked up at me
willing me to lean down to listen:
I made it out of the forest, out of the dark.

I scooped it up with an old wooden spoon,
folded it into my apron, set it gently
in the basket of my bicycle.
It beat quietly, watching the road ahead,
the birch trees becoming whiter as they closed in,
the outline of moose on guard
in the dark spaces behind the road's edges.

At home, placed on the kitchen table
in the center of all things,
in a straw basket lined with soft cotton pajamas,
she lay watching and breathing.
I sprinkled her with warm slightly-salted water
every hour as I came in and out,
laundry, toys, groceries, a new broom.

Her body pulsed as if she remembered something,
a familiarity, curved spaces, odd noises.
I have never been out in the air,
this could make me quite giddy
I could hear her words, her whispers
and sometimes even a hum.
I asked her if she wanted some lunch:
No, she said, *just you.*

You, Then, Later

*A circular tube clay fragment, 2 cm. long, from 1400 BC,
was found in Jerusalem bearing the ancient form of writing known as
'Akkadian wedge script' with the words: <u>you,</u> <u>then</u>, <u>later</u>.*

Someone knew the letters, knew their shapes,
understood carving and memory.

Someone held a piece of damp clay
in his hands, a delicately curved tool

probably of wood
gathered by women, shaped by water and stone.

He worked quickly,
carving a message he carried

from the gods or the midwife,
someone who had said to him:

*Go to Arran and bring me
A handful of wheat seeds,*

*A bowl of dried figs,
A branch of tilio.*

*You may keep some,
But go first, we will talk later.*

The carver cut swift coiled arcs
and diagonally stroked lines

into divided columns.
He then rolled the clay

into a tiny tube, set it
in the sun

and in the afternoon,
sent it wrapped in lamb skin

to a woman who knew these letters
and knew that clay

carved in this way
could spell a secret
or a revolution.

This object has been temporarily removed

we move up the soundless stained marble stairs
in a Museum somewhere in Connecticut

notice empty spaces on the walls
unobtrusive notices beside them
this object has been temporarily removed

blank rectangles with edges
stained by heat and hands

we ask
what are we missing

is this particular one
the one

that will explain it all to us
pull all the others together
into a comprehensible whole

why isn't it here
what happened to it

did a child poke her finger
into the cheeks

of the woman
with the yellow and purple head-dress

did an elderly gentleman
lean too close to the glass
his breath a bit greasy

did hot water dribble down the wall
from the rusted toilet pipes

did they find out
that it was a fake

did someone reclaim it
from a war

Perhaps if we had been able
to *see* it

we could have finally gone home
with quieter hearts

played with the waiting dog
eaten potato chips

stopped worrying that there was something else
we should be doing

and something more we should know about

As Good a Time as Any

Perhaps this would be
as good a time as any to die.

Carmina Burana blowing
the car windows out,
a chorus exploding through the roof,
my voice towering
in the midst of the ecstatic sound
as I drive through a day as beautiful as any,
fields of bent and broken corn,
goldenrod blossoms tenderly stroking
the dry and tired stalks.

The children are all fairly healthy,
a bit flabby around their middles,
pretty happy, good fathers,
haven't saved much money,
the grandchildren beautiful and smart.

My words are exactly
the same as yours
except in a different key,
mine D minor, yours F major,
a different hue, mine
the soundless snow filling the landscape,
yours, the heat bursting through clouds.

I think I have had the last
of your skin against my skin,
your warm naked chest
contoured against my back,

you turning me,
shifting and murmuring
to study my face,
stroke my hair back from my forehead.

At the next earthquake,
all the empty wine bottles
will fall off the top of the high wood cabinet
we never got around to varnishing,

cracked green and brown shards
flung against the red tiled floor,
random and dangerous,
a faint smell of soured fruit, decaying grass,
mice droppings and scorched light bulb sockets.

You no longer answer your phone,
you may be so sick you cannot

or your wife has instructed you not to,
but none of this makes any difference —

it might be as good a time as any

Before You Could Speak

Like the sound of breath / if your body left
        Christina Pugh, "Rotary"

In the Graveyard of the Souls
there is no telephone.
The Souls lie silently
beneath the thick, creased earth,
no markers, no remembrance.
We, creatures of the surface and the Heavens,
cannot reach them, even with surrender.

My mother is wearing a skirt that swirls around
        her legs.
She is standing in the back field near the
        asparagus bed
under the octagonal clothes line, the one
that circles around the central pole where I
        am standing.
I am leaning close to her, the top of my head
at her apron strings, drinking in her rhythm, her grace,
watching her snap the clothes to smooth them out
before hanging them on the thin, loops of rope
with the wooden clothes pegs
she holds between her teeth
in the sweet blueberry July air.

Pumpkins are scattered around the graveyard,
broken, split, fallen over.
No one has bothered to gather them.
They are of no concern to the Souls.
I eat the salty Greek olives and fat golden raisins
I tucked into my suitcase before flying over the Alps
and then across the body of silvered water
that separates us.

In December, in New Hampshire,
they taste, one by one,
like thin leaves and rising dust,
a fitting meal to ready the Soul for burial.

White Matter

Her collarbone filled with light when he told her
of the aging New York City subway cars hurled into
    the Atlantic
off the coast of Maryland in order to create
an artificial reef for marine life.

Later she saw fields of thistles, wild vines,
    mustard blossoms.
It rained mint, and she learned that the volume
    of white matter
in her brain would expand as soon as she learned
    to juggle.

She heard his skin pulsing with gratitude, noticed the sky
around his head vibrating in a frequency like stained glass.
His voice became *a line of perfect crystals without*
    a single blemish.

At dawn, the sea gull and the crow carried them to the land
between the sun and the moon where they watched the sun
drop color over oranges, blackberries, water.

She was all white, an elegy to unyielding space, dead men
    and wolves.
The sea turtles swam into the sound of years, imprinted
    with their return.
There was no end to what she saw and heard.

The Fugue

> *Our soul is escaped as a bird out of the snare of the fowlers:*
> *the snare is broken and we are escaped.*
> Psalms 124/7

I

This war, this time, has been too much.
We have lived many wars these years.
Our lives are war, you could say.
But this one has pushed me outside of myself.

Again, we fight, we run, we stand.
Again, we know how precarious
our survival, our homes.
Sometimes I cannot bear it,
other times, it is all I know.

The rockets came pouring down
out of the bright blue sky
and killed Amir right in front of us.
What could we tell the children?
Yes. Again. This is all they know.

We go on cooking eggplant,
buying soap, chickens, fava beans.
We stay in the back rooms
away from the mortar whine,
away from the cries, the treads.
The phone sputters.

This time, I cannot turn back.
I cannot. I am driven forward.
I will call her.

I will go to Tamar, she phoned
but I am afraid.
Not of her, but of the others.
Of the place we choose. And the hour,
the possibility of darkness.

Please come, please.
I need you, need to see your face,
your hands, hear your words.
Please.

       II

Two women meet,
bend toward each other
and then away,
loving and uncertainty shudder
inside the membranes
of memory and terror.

Bodies mirror each other,
white arms reach out,
fold back,

one son lost, one husband gone,
black dresses, pomegranates choreographing
their mourning.

Search my face, my eyes,
we are the hope,
the ibis and the spoonbill,
the blue-cheeked bee-eater and the peregrine falcon
that will finally return once again to our lands.

Their necks curve like swans at night,
their shadows on the walls,
great hooded hawks.
Flocks of starlings hover,
their bare feet tremble.

They whisper of Rebecca,
remember the lemon trees
and lying down in front of the tanks
after school.
And what their fathers said later.

The mine that exploded
in front of their houses
blowing the asphalt to bits,
dogs, carts, bicycles,
unrecognizable fragments.

The secret lunch they had
at that tiny cafe high above the city
where they shook off their sandals,
feet sore from walking and heat,
the Moroccan waiter tenderly placing
newspaper under their bare feet.

Do not forget what we learned
in sixth grade, how segments of Chopin
were broadcast on clandestine radio frequencies
every thirty seconds in Prague in 1939
to give courage, inspiration and unity
to the men and women of the Polish Resistance
against the Nazi occupation.

III

The treacherous oleander
circles their languages, their syllables,
cicadas sizzle in the heat,
thickets of bamboo too dense
for a path toward redemption.

Yellow has been the color
of the first blossoms of spring
as long as we can remember.
This spring no yellow flowers appeared
in the fields, the gardens, the hillsides.

But we will exchange skin,
you will wear mine, I yours,
and we will bring back the yellows,
then the reds, the purples
and finally the whites.

Written after viewing *Strategic Alliance #4*, oil on canvas by Hayes Friedman

About the Author

Becky Dennison Sakellariou was born and raised in the United States outside of Boston, Massachusetts, and in 1965, she moved to Greece where she married, settled and thrived for more than forty years. Her professional work has included teaching, writing, editing and counseling. Sakellariou's attachment to Greece and her abiding roots in New England have given her the gift of two singular perspectives on peoples, cultures, geography and daily living which inhabit and enrich Sakellariou's writing.

Sakellariou has written and published poetry for many years; her chapbook, *The Importance of Bone,* won first prize in the Blue Light Press (San Francisco) competition of 2005 and her full-length book, *Earth Listening*, was published in 2010 by Hobblebush Books of Brookline, NH. In 2013, Finishing Line Press (Tennessee) brought out her chapbook, *What Shall I Cry?,* which was followed by a two-year long collaboration with Greek poet, Maria Laina, for *The Possibility of Red/Η Πιθανοτιτα του Κοκκινου,* a bilingual edition of eleven of her poems, also published by Hobblebush Books. In 2015, Passager Books (Baltimore) brought out her art/poetry book, *Gathering the Soft,* a meditation on cancer illustrated by Tandy Zorba. Sakellariou's latest book, *No Foothold in this Geography,* is a collection of the last five years of her work.

In the past few years, world political events have empowered Sakellariou's writing, infusing it with tension, contradiction and even ambiguity. Most recently, her attention has been centered around the refugee situation in Europe, specifically Turkey and Greece, and her own experiences in the camps and with the immigrants themselves. Her poetry reflects her endless amazement at both the power of memory and the persistence of the mystery of all things. ϒ

www.beckysakellariou.com

Made in the USA
Lexington, KY
28 September 2018